# VENICE

Designed and Produced by

Ted Smart & David Gibbon

MAYFLOWER BOOKS · NEW YORK CITY

# Introduction

VENICE is one of the wonders of the modern world: a truly lovely city, on every tourist's list of Essential Places to visit in Europe, and one of the few cities which has been able almost to ignore some of the least attractive aspects of twentieth-century life. True, motorized water taxis and vaporettos buzz up and down and across the Grand Canal, since 1846 there has been a railway and since 1931 a causeway for motor vehicles linking Venice to the Italian mainland. But no modern blocks of flats or offices have reared up amidst the Renaissance and Baroque palaces, no bulldozer has smashed its way through centuries-old squares and narrow back waters to make way for concrete shopping precincts or multi-story car parks.

There is one car park and garage in the Piazzale Roma, at the end of the causeway from the mainland, and there the visitor must leave his car. For – greatest twentieth-century wonder of all – Venice has no cars.

Venice is a city of quiet and calm. She seems to float on gently rippling water in a pool of peace and serenity where the loudest sounds – apart from the motor boats on the Grand Canal – may be a concerted flapping of wings in St Mark's Square as clouds of pigeons suddenly rise into the air together; or the peal, chime and gong of bells from one or more of Venice's hundreds of churches and bell towers; or the warning cry of a gondolier as he manoeuvres his elegant, black-painted craft under a bridge or round a corner.

The gondola and its owner are perhaps the most immediately obvious link with Venice's past. Step into one and, if you are imaginative, you can feel instantly transported back across the centuries. There have been gondolas on the canals for nearly a thousand years. No great painter of the Venetian scene has omitted them from his work: Canaletto, Carpaccio in his *Story of St Ursula,* even Gentile Bellini in his painting of *The Miracle of the Cross,* all managed to include the gondola.

In their time, gondolas were the main means of transport round Venice's miles of canals. Today, although they are occasionally used for transporting goods, along with their pretty relative, the sandolo, which one may see delivering milk or bread in back canals, they are largely a tourist attraction, though the gondoliers themselves are very much a part of Venetian life.

Like most Venetians, much of their lives revolve round the tourist season, for without the tourists and their purses, Venice could not survive. So the Venetians have to work extra hard in the few months the tourists are there, to get themselves and their families through the damp, cold and foggy winter; and a rather bizarre, phrenetic layer of human activity is laid over the impression of quiet tranquility the city itself manages to convey.

Behind the discreetly closed shutters of the houses, whole families will push themselves, at great inconvenience, into half their usual living space to leave rooms free for letting to visitors. The tourist in his gondola will find himself jostling for position on the crowded waters of the Grand Canal with the water buses, motor boats and fishing craft which also use Venice's main street. If he sits for a quiet coffee in one of the cafés in St Mark's Square, he will hear the band of his café playing tunes from Edwardian or 1920's musical comedies, while across the square, another band is in competition with something jazzier. The Venetians themselves will not sit on either side but prefer to walk down the middle, hearing both bands and watching the tourists paying exorbitant sums for very small coffees.

Some of the workshops down obscure side streets also produce goods aimed largely at the visitor. Some specialize in making antique-looking, heavily ornate gilt frames to hold recently-painted pictures in the style of Guardi or Canaletto. Not that all the paintings look recently done. The men who paint them are very skilled at giving them the patina of age, and if someone is foolish enough to pay considerably more for them than they are worth, thinking he has made a great artistic discovery in that obscure back street, then that is his business. Other workshops make hand-made shoes, and will sell them for less than they would fetch in the shops in the center of town, if the buyer is prepared to bargain with the makers. Amid piles of wood shavings and the smell of glue, others make furniture, some in ornate old-fashioned styles, some with simple modern lines. Much of these wares spill out onto the pavements and are allowed to pile up against the walls.

There is little that the Venetians do not know about the history and architecture of their own city, and if they do not know something, they are unlikely to admit it. Pity the poor tourists who get a Venetian guide in love with one room in the Doge's Palace. He will go on and on, pointing out every detail of every picture, every carved piece of every square yard of painted ceiling, oblivious to the boredom, cricked necks and sore feet of his party. But he does it because he genuinely does not want you to miss anything of his wonderful city. Ask someone the way somewhere and he may just point up the alley in front of you, but he may also come with you to make sure you do not miss it or to point out other items of interest on the way.

The clever visitor to Venice will arm himself with a map and take himself round the city. He will probably yield once to the blandishments of the gondoliers – and if he is romantic, he will do so in the evening when the sunset is turning the buildings grey, pink and gold, and the lights from the palazzos are beginning to glow on the darkening water – just to say that he has been on a Venetian gondola, and after that he will save his lire and travel by vaporetto, along with the thrifty Venetians.

*The white dome of the church of Santa Maria della Salute can be seen to the right of the picture of the Grand Canal illustrated on* pages 4 and 5.

*The inside of St Mark's Basilica from the central nave is shown* left *with a spectacular succession of cupolas, galleries and arches. From the cupola of the Pentecost hangs the Byzantine cross, its eight arms illuminated on solemn occasions by a hundred flickering candles.*

Or he will walk, for despite all those canals, back-water, and water-filled dead ends – 'Streets full of water. Please advise', Robert Benchley cabled home to America when he arrived for the first time in Venice – the city is easy to walk around. A first glance at a map of the city may suggest that its streets and canals form a monstrous labyrinth, but once its layout has been mastered, few parts of it will be found to be much more than twenty minutes away from anywhere else, and most parts are certainly worth discovering.

Venice is an old city, and much of it looks it – foundations crumbling from the action of the waters in which they sit, plaster peeling off walls, towers leaning at odd angles. But it is not a dead city. Very few, even of the oldest buildings which may date back to the thirteenth century, are left to molder away. The Venetians make full use of their past in their present. The Customs building (Dogana) has been used as such since the fifteenth century, ships were being repaired at the Arsenal in Dante's time and still are today. Other centuries-old buildings have been put to more modern uses – perhaps as a cinema, a bar, a post office or a shop.

The main shopping streets have been so for centuries. The direct route from St Mark's Square to the Rialto, once the business heart of Venice, is the same today as when Shylock, in his Jewish gaberdine, walked there. The main street on the route is still the Merceria del Orologio. Orologio, which leads directly out of St Mark's Square under the fifteenth century Clock Tower is the really smart and expensive street, where the best leather, the best glass, the smartest accessories may be found. Once past the Church of St Julian and on your way to the Rialto, you find in Merceria the more everyday things and the tourist souvenirs – black plastic music boxes shaped like gondolas, plastic paperweights shaped like the Campanile, scarves painted with the insignia of Venice, or extraordinarily grotesque glassware it would be easy to call vulgar, but is perhaps more easily understood as part of the streak of theatricality and Commedia dell' Arte which runs right through Venetian history and life.

Shakespeare's Shylock and his ship-merchant adversary, Antonio, would probably not much care for the Rialto today. They would not even recognize the Rialto Bridge, as the present one was not built until late in the sixteenth century. They would find a few banks, but the great commercial center of their day has given way to vegetable and fish markets. True, the fish market which lies around the corner of the Rialto Bridge on the Grand Canal is one of the great early morning sights of Venice. But it could hardly be expected to excite men who had dealt in the spices, jewels, silks and gold of the Levant, and who had heard the decrees of the most powerful mercantile empire since the Ancient Greeks, promulgated from the pedestal of the *Gobbo di Rialto*. The Gobbo stone is still to be seen, but looking rather forlorn.

They might feel more at home if they explored the buildings on the Grand Canal, both up and downstream from the Rialto Bridge, for several of them date from the fourteenth and fifteenth centuries: the Ca' d'Oro, for instance, which now contains the Franchetti art gallery, and which is typical of the classical Venetian civic architecture, was built in the fifteenth century; the Fondaco dei Tedeschi, now the city's central post and telegraph office,

was built in 1505, and is one of several former warehouses still in use; the gothic Palazzo Segredo was built at the end of the fourteenth century, and the Palazzo dei Camerlengh was completed in 1528.

The Grand Canal, as the main artery of Venice, is lined on both sides with splendid buildings, many of them the former palaces of the Venetian nobility, families whose names were recorded in the Golden Book. But the Grand Canal does not have a monopoly on grand buildings in Venice, for the Venetian nobility did not confine itself to one quarter – there is no 'Mayfair' in Venice – and their palaces may be found in almost any part of the city, often with beautiful gardens hidden away behind high walls and overlooked by the apartment houses and washing lines of lesser citizens. Gardens may sometimes be seen growing at the tops of houses, too, for many Venetians not blessed with gardens around their houses have built their own on terraces and roof-tops.

The visitor to Venice, strolling from one to another of her 118 islands over canals crossed by more than 400 bridges, and passing several of her 107 churches in his walk, could not fail to notice that the Venetians like detail. Not for them the smooth, flat slabs of concrete of modern architecture, or even the simple grace of English Georgian. Few buildings in Venice are allowed to go unadorned. They may have been brightened up with a birdcage on the balcony or with a few simple pots of geraniums on windowsills and ledges, or, at the other extreme, they may have been adorned with whole, elaborately carved menageries of animals and birds or with coats of arms and family crests, angels and Madonnas, crusaders, even people in boats. And everywhere, of course, is the winged lion of St Mark, sometimes with his paw on an open book on which is inscribed '*Pax tibi, Marce, Evangelista meus*'. The writer, E. V. Lucas, once stopped to count the lions on the Porta della Carta. There were 75 of them.

St Mark and his lion, which now dominate Venice, did not appear on the scene until four centuries after the foundation of the city, the traditional date for which is 421 AD.

Whether or not this date is accurate, it was certainly during the fifth and sixth centuries that the settlement that was to become Venice grew out of the marshy lagoons on the northern Adriatic shore of Italy, built by people fleeing the barbaric tribes which over-ran Italy when the Roman Empire fell apart. In the Lagoon, the refugees found a measure of safety. In time, they forgot their land-based origins and became used to living on and being surrounded by water. Set apart from Italy, the city came under the influence of Byzantium, and her first laws and the election of the first Doge, in 697, were all approved by Byzantium.

The Venice we know today began to take shape in the ninth century, when the seat of government was moved from Torcello to the Rialto. By this time, the Venetians were sure enough of their future importance in the world to realize that they needed a patron saint who could wield a greater influence in their affairs than the obscure Greek saint, Theodore, who had hitherto been the city's patron saint. Thus St Mark first appeared in the life of Venice.

Legend had it that St Mark had voyaged to the northern Adriatic where a great storm had wrecked his boat and washed him ashore. An angel then appeared to him in a vision saying 'Pax tibi . . .' The Venetians decided that this meant that St Mark must be allowed to find peace in Venice. In 828 two of their number stole his remains from his tomb in Alexandria and brought them in triumph to Venice. The next year a great basilica was begun, to house the relics of the Saint.

Today, as they were for hundreds of years when Venice went to war under the banner of St Mark, the saint's winged lion and open book are still the great symbols of the city. Poor St Theodore was relegated to the background, although there is a statue of him standing, no-one knows why, on a crocodile, prominently displayed on one of the two columns which mark the entrance to the city in the Piazzetta of St Mark. On the other column is the familiar winged lion, this one a bronze version from the East which spent some time in Paris after Napoleon conquered the city in 1797. The lion was eventually returned, damaged, to Venice and put back on its column.

When Napoleon conquered Venice, he was merely giving the *coup de grace* to a state which had been decaying and moribund for centuries. Venice achieved greatness because her geographical position allowed her to benefit from the movement of world trade. In the Middle Ages the riches of the East came overland to Turkey and the Eastern Mediterranean. Venice made it her business to insure that it was the ships owned by the Venetian state which had a monopoly in transporting the Eastern goods to Venice and on to the rest of Europe.

But in 1453 Constantinople fell to the Turks and Venice's imperial influence there came to an end. Then in 1492 Christopher Columbus discovered America, and with it a whole new world from which Venice, at the wrong end of the Adriatic, could not benefit. A few years later Vasco da Gama made his way round the Cape of Good Hope and charted a new sea route to the East, from which the Atlantic nations, not Venice, would gain. So sensitive were the Venetians to the importance of the Eastern overland route to their prosperity, that within two days of receiving the news of da Gama's feat in 1499, several Rialto banks failed. Five years later Venice suggested to the Sultan that a canal should be cut through the Isthmus of Suez, but to no avail. Venice's long decline had begun.

When Napoleon sent his troops to Venice, she was a moribund state, her nobility effete and the city given over to masquerades, mindless pleasures and carnivals. Napoleon was not impressed. He got rid of the last Doge, Ludovico Manin, with contemptuous ease, and burned the Golden Book – the ancient rolls of the nobility which since 1287 had listed the names of the only Venetians who might hold office in the state. Venice was ceded to Austria for a time, came back under French rule until 1815, then under Austrian again until 1866, when she was united with the Italian kingdom and became just another city in the new nation.

Much of this history can be traced in St Mark's Square itself. You need hardly stir from your comfortable seat in fashionable Florian's cafe, on the south side of the Square, to see much of it. To your right are the great Basilica of St Mark itself – not the one begun in 829 as this was destroyed by fire in 976, rebuilt then demolished and begun again in 1063; a corner of the Doge's Palace; and the massive bell tower, or Campanile, which is comparatively recent, having been rebuilt in 1912 as an exact replica of the campanile which had stood there for centuries until it collapsed in 1902. On the opposite side of the Square, to the right, is the Clock Tower, crowned by the great bell which, struck by two figures of Moors, has been sounding the time for four and a half centuries. Next to it is the Procuratie Vecchie, with its two elegant floors of loggias, which was begun in the fifteenth century as a house for the 'procurators', or magistrates, in charge of the Basilica. Florian's cafe is itself under the arches of the other procurator's house, the Procurate Nuove. At the western end of the Square lies visible evidence of Napoleon's influence in Venice: the Ala Napoleonica, or Fabbrica Nuova, built on the site of Sansovino's Church of San Geminiano, which Napoleon tore down.

The squares of Venice – St Mark's is the only one to be called 'piazza'; the rest are 'campi' or 'campielli' – are to Venetians what the pub is to the Englishman: places to meet friends and neighbours, to pass the time of day over a drink at the cafe, to greet the priest as he walks over the square to the church, ignoring or quietly smiling at the fact that some boys are using a wall of his church as a goal for their game of soccer. There will be pigeons in the square, for pigeons are much-indulged birds in Venice, having been closely linked with the history and legends of the city since earliest times. In St Mark's Square there is an official pigeon-feeder who comes out with grain for the birds twice a day, summer and winter.

And, of course, there are cats – long, lean, elegant cats prowling about the tables of the cafés, lounging on windowsills, in stairways and on balconies. English people are apt to think them ill-fed, even starving, and have been known to write long series of letters to The Times newspaper about them. But on the whole the Venetian cats are all right. They may not be loved by all Venetians, but it has become a case of live and let live – and, anyway, they keep the mice at bay.

The Venetians themselves have been good at keeping things at bay – water, decay, tourists, the rest of the world. A prosaic characteristic, at odds with the extraordinary beauty of their surroundings, but perhaps a good one. It allowed Venice to develop with a glorious uniqueness:

A 'sun-girt City, thou has been
Ocean's child, and then his queen.'

*At the far limits of St Mark's Piazzetta is located St Mark's Wharf overleaf with its two granite columns brought from the Orient, in 1172, by Niccolo Barattieri. The left hand column is surmounted by a statue of San Teodoro, the first protector of the Venetians, and the right hand column by a bronze statue of the Lion of St Mark, a symbol of both St Mark the Evangelist and the power of the Venetian Republic.*

12

*The beautiful square of St Mark's is shown below, the Bell Tower left, the Clock Tower below right and the Procuratie Vecchie above.*

*Illustrated overleaf is the color-washed church of San Giorgio on the island of San Giorgio Maggiore.*

The original Basilica of St Mark's above and left, dating from 829, was built by the Doge Giustignano Partecipazio to house the mortal remains of St Mark the Evangelist, the patron saint of the city. Destroyed by fire, it was rebuilt between 1043 and 1071 by the Doge Domenico Conterini and follows the design of Byzantine churches in the plan of a Greek cross, although interpreted in the romanesque style. The present Basilica incorporates Byzantine, Gothic, Islamic and Renaissance architecture.

The beautiful sculptures of the upper story, by the Florentine, Lamberti, are shown in detail right and were executed by the sculptor in the 15th century.

Depicting the 'Universal Judgement' the exquisite mosaic overleaf is displayed over the principal portal of the Basilica and is the work of L. Querena.

The design of the Euganean trachyte pavement in St Mark's Square, with its geometrical white bands, illustrated above and left, *was planned by the architect, Andrea Tirali, in 1723. Today it provides a vast open-air concert hall* below *and, with its open-air cafés* right and above left *is a meeting place for both the Venetians themselves and for tourists from all over the world.*

Suffused in a golden glow from the sun's last rays, St Mark's overleaf *stands majestically as night enfolds the Basilica.*

# A Window to the East

VENICE made her fortune and built up her enormous power in the Middle Ages because she looked eastwards to Turkey, the Levant and the Indies, rather than to mainland Italy and western Europe. In her origins, Venice was more of the east than of the west; a cluster of islands in a lagoon; deliberately setting herself apart from the rest of Italy, she looked towards the old Roman Empire of Byzantium for protection and aid. For several centuries, Venice's tribunes came under the authority of the Roman Emperor's viceroy at Ravenna.

In time, Venice no longer needed the protection or help of the crumbling Empire, and used it for her own ends. The Christian Crusades to the Holy Lands, aimed at ridding them of the influence of the Infidel, were a glorious opportunity for gaining wealth which the Venetians grasped firmly. Doges and Senators agreed to ship the Crusaders and their supplies to the Levant, but always at a price highly advantageous to the Venetians.

When Venice finally joined in a Crusade herself – the Fourth – it was with the intention of winning as much as she could out of the former Byzantium, now the Christian city of Constantinople. Ignoring the city's religion, and attacking her during Holy Week in 1204, Venice grabbed the richest 'quarter and a half-quarter' of the Empire, including its best ports. Byzantine gold poured into Venice, Venetian merchants enjoyed privileges of trade in the eastern ports not given to Levantine merchants, and her ships sailed the great sea routes unhindered as they visited the ports of the Levant, taking on cargoes from Arabia, Persia, Afghanistan and India. Back home on the Rialto, her merchants sat beside a great map showing the major routes of their commerce and counted the gains from trading in wines, spices, silks, velvets, gold and jewels.

But trade was not the only factor linking Venice with the East. The instincts of her people seemed to lie in that direction rather than towards the west. The Venetian explorer, Marco Polo, chose to travel east overland to China, and came back with such tales as to fire his compatriots' imaginations for generations. It might have been better for the future of Venice if he had gone west; he might have found the routes to the Americas and round Africa which were to decide who would be the powerful nations of the post-renaissance world.

The Venetian delight in ceremony and display had a distinctly oriental flavour about it, particularly when set in the Piazza of St Mark against the facade of the Basilica. The love of rich cloths and gorgeous colors – crimson, gold and purple (itself a dye from the East), the delight in ritual and procession, the use of jewels to stud ornaments and even paintings, all smack of the opulence of the orient.

St Mark's Basilica itself has little of the European cathedral about it, but a great deal of the oriental mosque. Its form is that of the Greek cross. Its domes, its marble veneers, its rich use of mosaics and, above all, the great treasures it contains, all signal the Eastern influence in Venice. Even the Basilica's reason for existence is based on having received the remains of the Evangelist Mark from their resting place in Alexandria in Egypt.

Many of St Mark's most famous treasures came from the sack of Constantinople, or were the gifts of merchants and captains bringing precious objects home from the East to beautify Venice's great temple.

Among them are the four bronze horses which stood for centuries over the main entrance, and which once graced the Hippodrome in Constantinople; parts of the breathtaking Pala d'Oro (Reredos), which is made up of individual Byzantine plaques mounted in gold and encrusted with jewels; a glass goblet mounted in gold filigree ornamented with enamels and precious stones; the icon of the Madonna Nicopeia, which many Venetians believe can work miracles; the icon of the Archangel Michael; and the four little porphyry Moors, or Tetrarchs, which look down from the outside of the Basilica, on the side next to the Doge's Palace. No-one is quite sure who these four figures represent or why they should stand, hands on sword hilts, with their arms about each others' shoulders. The figures, which may be the four Tetrarchs of Diocletian, are thought to have come originally from Syria or Egypt.

There are other figures of Moors in Venice, most notably the two – naked but for skin loin cloths – who strike the hours on the bell of the Clock Tower on the other side of the Piazza. By the eighteenth century, the figures of Moors had degenerated into black page boys, turbanned and bejewelled, and used to hold lanterns or flambeaux. Such figures have recently enjoyed a vogue among antique dealers in Europe and America.

St Mark's Basilica is probably the most obviously Byzantine building left in Venice, but traces of the orient can still be seen in many other buildings, overlaid with Gothic and the Venetian Renaissance styles. The Fondaco dei Turchi, which dates from the mid-thirteenth century, though it was heavily restored in the nineteenth, perhaps shows its Arab and Byzantine origins better than other buildings in the city. The name 'warehouse of the Turks' is not a pointer to style: the Turks were rented the old palace in the seventeenth century as a storehouse for their goods.

There are other aspects of the East which may still be felt, rather than seen, in Venice today. It is very much a matter of atmosphere. Visit the damp and gloomy *Piombi*, the old prisons of the Doge's Palace, and you feel more than a hint of oriental inscrutability about their grim and empty silence. Or stand on the Riva degli Schiavoni and breathe in the sea-laden air. Is there a hint of spices, of the scents of Arabia there as well? Certainly, the Venetians would think so, for they see their city as a bridge between east and west; for them the East begins on the shores of the Serenissima.

*Gondolas and small power boats ply the canalways right where the crumbling, stuccoed houses teeter on the water's edge.*

The Grand Canal, the main artery of Venice, is lined with splendid buildings, illustrated on these pages and overleaf, *many of which were former palaces of the Venetian nobility. Spanning the canal is the beautiful Rialto Bridge* below left, *the work of Antonio da Ponte and built between 1588 and 1591, which links the Riva del Carbon (Bank of Coal) with the Riva del Vin (Bank of Wine).*

27

The origin of the gondola dates from the 11th century, when it was considerably larger and manoeuvred by twelve oarsmen. Sumptuously decorated in the 16th and 17th centuries, it has since been simplified to become the characteristic and elegant boat shown above, below, right and on page 34, and, together with the traditionally dressed gondoliers, constitutes an indispensable element of Venetian tourism.

Pretty bridges form necessary links between the high walled houses across the narrower waterways left, and overleaf the high dome of the church of Santa Maria della Salute dominates the skyline in the picturesque view of the Grand Canal.

# The World of the Golden Book

HOW paradoxical seems the government of Venice in her golden days when seen from the more politically cut-and-dried twentieth century.

Here was a city of pageantry and rich splendors, the most cosmopolitan in Europe, where citizens of almost any country in the known world mingled freely on the Rialto, Europe's busiest money market, and site, too, of its most famous bawdy house: a city where the rich merchants built their palaces with room underneath for their warehouses, and where the courtesans were so renowned that even visiting kings were taken to meet the greatest of them and to discuss poetry and art.

It was a state, too, whose citizens were tightly ruled by a patrician oligarchy who could try and condemn in private anyone accused of a crime, sometimes simply on the basis of an anonymous accusation dropped into one of several Lion's Mouths (Bocca del Leone) dotted about the city, and who guarded the state's assets so stringently that even a humble glass-maker leaving Venice without permission would be pursued and killed. No outsider must be allowed to learn the secrets behind a Venetian monopoly, even one as apparently innocuous, though very lucrative, as glass-making.

For eleven hundred years the titular head of the Venetian Republic, and the only official appointed for life, was the Doge. The first in a long line, Paolucci Anafesto, was elected in 697. In 1797, Napoleon forced the last one, Ludovico Manin, to abdicate.

The early doges were leaders in fact as well as in title, though the Venetians seldom allowed them to become too ambitious or powerful. Of the first fifty, the reigns of nineteen ended in murder, banishment, deposition or mutilation. While Venice was still under Byzantine influence, the punishment meted out to several doges was truly frightful: they were blinded over live coals. Others fled to the sanctuary of monasteries to avoid such fates.

The style of Venetian government took its course towards oligarchy with a decree of 1297 which barred the ordinary citizen from taking part in government and handed over power to the members of patrician families who had sat on the Great Council and whose names were inscribed in the Golden Book. Real power was held by magistrates, none of whom could hold their office for long, sitting in committees, each of which kept a check on the others. There was a Signory, a Collegio, a council to administer justice, another to watch over the Navy, and another for the Arsenal and the state's massive ship-building industry which furnished a 3000-strong fleet of ships. There was also the Council of Ten and later, the Council of Three – the most feared councils of all.

In time, the doge, stripped of his powers, became a figurehead, richly apparelled on state occasions and in his person almost sacred, but in private almost a prisoner in his gorgeous palace, limited in the amount of money he might spend, lest he appear too extravagant or too mean; unable to send or receive a letter without it being seen and approved by his counsellors; unable even to leave the city except in exceptional circumstances.

So, until Napoleon came along five hundred years later, Venice was to be ruled by an anonymous, committee-ridden patrician oligarchy. Decisions might be taken slowly but, once taken, they were acted on with swift, silent efficiency. Ordinary Venetians might know little of them until the dreadful consequences were put before them: perhaps the corpse of a strangled man found floating in the Lagoon, or strung up by one leg to a gibbet in the Piazzetta, with no explanation of who they were or why they had been so treated. So many prisoners walked to oblivion over the bridge linking the State Inquisitors' office in the Doge's Palace to the prison, that it came to be called the Bridge of Sighs.

The Bridge has not changed today. You can see it from the Riva degli Schiavoni, linking the first floors of the two buildings: a pretty bridge, its ornamentation giving the impression of white sugar icing and its windows covered with marble trellising to preserve the anonymity of victim and judge.

And yet – another aspect of the Venetian paradox – the citizens of Venice knew a freedom not granted to many during the Middle Ages and Renaissance. Government might be strict, but it was exercised with justice and it guaranteed a measure of security to all. The state had a systematic way of pensioning retired servants, and widows and orphans were provided for. The noble families were educated to be rulers, not rich dilettantes, and were required to serve their state as administrators, diplomats, judges and warriors. They did not have titles; only in the nineteenth century did the Austrians devise a system of titles for the Venetians under their rule.

At a time when anti-semitism was widespread in Europe, Jews lived and worked in peace in Venice. The Jews in their ghetto – a word first used in Venice and thought to come from *gettare*, to smelt bronze – were just one, though the most strictly controlled by the state, of many communities into which Venetians were divided, each of which had its own head and a measure of autonomy.

The state was also so tolerant towards Lutherans and anti-papal Catholics that many Europeans, including Sir Henry Wotton, King James I of England's ambassador to Venice, thought that the city would itself turn Protestant.

Although the Golden Book was burned on the orders of Napoleon, traces of the way of life it symbolized are still very much in evidence in Venice today. The Doge's Palace, which was parliament and government offices as well as residence, is still there, facing the Lagoon and St Mark's Square; the Ghetto Nuovo and its tall, narrow houses still face silently inwards, gloomy and rather despairing; and past commercial wealth and mercantile power can still be traced among the palaces and former warehouses which line the Grand Canal.

More than this, Venice still carries an intangible presence of power and conviction. More than just another Italian city, she has an aura which tells you that the meaning of her existence was power, not just pretty architecture.

*Draped in verdant creepers and banked with colorful blooms the elegant houses overleaf line the banks of the canal.*

Gondolas overleaf and footbridges, such as the typical example illustrated left, leading to one of a number of cramped back streets, are essential in Venice, which, with its narrow canals makes it necessary to travel within the city by canal or on foot.

The Church of San Vidal above was founded in the 11th century, the main body of the present building having been designed by Gaspari in the 17th century and the façade completed by Andrea Tirali at the beginning of the 18th.

Across the tiled roof tops the Church of San Giovanni e Paolo above right stands out against a clear blue sky, while below right the houses in the small square shine in the bright primary colors reminiscent of a child's painting.

The monument below commemorates the patriot, Paolo Sarpi (c. 1552–1623), a scholar and state theologian, who, as an early Italian advocate of church-state separatism and author of a book decrying papal absolutism, played a dominant role in his support of the Republic during Venice's struggle with Pope Paul V.

*The pretty canal scenes shown on these pages and overleaf illustrate the charm of Venice with her quaint buildings rising from the gently undulating sun-dappled waters, while above right can be seen the Ca'Minelli "Del Bovolo" stairway, a curious Lombard spiral staircase designed by Giovanni Candi in 1500.*

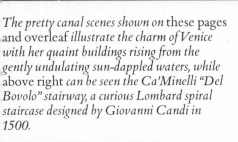

43

# Festivals and Fetes

PAGEANTRY, rituals, feasts and fêtes have always played a part in the life of Venice. Far from being just 'bread and circuses' to keep the people quiet, in the Ancient Roman style, they have been more a demonstration to the rest of the world of the power and importance of Venice's place in it, and of the pride of her citizens in their state.

Guilds, religious brotherhoods, the gondoliers' fraternity, knights in armour, the strolling players who gave the world Harlequin and Puncinella, even gymnasts, fist fighters and acrobats, all contributed to the Venetian pageant.

In his well-known painting of a Corpus Christi Procession in St Mark's Square, Gentile Bellini painted the scene in loving detail: the ranks of the religious brotherhoods in white robes, noble young men in striped hose, merchants in long gowns, banners waving, censers swaying in the hands of the bearers. It is a rich procession, planned with precision and set against the golden backdrop of the Basilica of St Mark.

The greatest pageantry surrounded the doges. Each one marked the beginning of his reign with a great procession in St Mark's Square. Carried above the crowds by a band of workers from the Arsenal, he would scatter coins to the throng. When Francesco Foscari was elected doge in 1423, the feasts and pageants he arranged to mark the occasion went on for a whole year.

The pageantry arranged to impress the young king Henry III of France when he visited Venice in 1574 was on such a lavish scale that the king was said to have never completely recovered his equilibrium afterwards. The great artists of the day – Palladio, Tintoretto and Veronese – designed and decorated the triumphal arches of welcome, the great state barge which bore the king into the city was rowed by 400 Slav oarsmen, and there was an escort of fourteen galleys plus a huge raft on which the glass-blowers of Venice showed their skill as they were drawn along.

For eight centuries the most important event in the doge's year, as it was of Venice's, was the Ascension Day ceremony of Venice's marriage to the sea. It had begun as a simple pouring of a libation into the sea by Doge Pietro Orseolo as he received the blessing of the Patriarch of Venice before leaving the safety of the Lagoon for the Adriatic on his way to defeat the Dalmations in 997. Later, the ceremony came to symbolize Venice's mercantile power. 'O sea, we wed thee in sign of our true and everlasting dominion,' declared the doge as he threw a gold ring into the sea from the deck of his magnificent gold and crimson state barge, the *Bucentaur*.

Today, the Ascension is marked in Venice at the Clock Tower in St Mark's Square. Only in Ascension Week, figures of the three Magi of the New Testament, accompanied by a herald angel, come out on the hour and do homage to the Madonna. The little ceremony is watched, not by religious figures or robed merchants, but by tourists of all nationalities, cameras clicking and necks craning for a better view. When it is over, they return to buying postcards from one of the sellers who have been given a license to trade in the Square, or to taking tea or drinking coffee seated at the neatly arranged rows of tables and chairs outside Florian's or Quadri's, the two famous cafés of the Square.

Pageantry and display still play a big part in the Venetian year. There are regattas in which boatmen from the six *sestieri* take part, candle-lit religious processions in the churches, the great Biennale art festival, and the annual international film festival on the Lido.

Some of the events are very much the work of the tourist authorities, keeping things lively for the visitors; there are regular band concerts in St Mark's Square, for instance, a Feast of Lights on the Grand Canal at the height of the tourist season in August, and regular floating concerts with gondoliers vying with each other to see who can sing sentimental Neapolitan, rather than Venetian, songs with most feeling.

The Feast of the Redentore remains as a truly characteristic Venetian festival. It celebrates one of Venice's many recoveries from the plague, and takes place on the eve of Redemption Sunday each July. For the occasion, a bridge on Pontoons is thrown across the wide stretch of the Giudecca Canal to the Church of the Redentore, boats gaily be-decked and sparkling with lanterns jostle on the water, and a gloriously colorful fireworks display turns the water, the sky and the buildings red and gold, green and orange. It is as if the plague departed only yesterday, rather than three hundred years ago, so fresh is the excitement.

It is a tradition of this festival that, once the fireworks are over, you should cross the water to the Lido, there to watch Nature's own display of colors in the sunrise; you might also care to bathe in the Lagoon before returning home to bed.

Relief from the plague is also celebrated in November in Venice, this time at special thanksgiving services at the Church of the Salute. Perhaps Venice has reason to be thankful still to Santa Maria della Salute: in the last great plague to devastate Venice – it ended in November 1631 after raging for sixteen months – eighty-two thousand people died.

Another Venetian event not to be missed is the Regatta, an immensely colorful occasion many consider more exciting to watch than Siena's famous horse race, the Palio.

Certainly, it empties the streets and squares of the city as everyone manoeuvres for a vantage point on the Grand Canal, on balconies, along the banks and the Riva degli Schiavoni and in boats moored along the edges of the Canal.

The regattas are the occasions when Venetians bring out the *bissona,* which are eight-oared boats, brilliantly decorated and rowed by men in rich costumes of silks, satins and Burano lace. The oars are striped red and white, flags are unfurled, the sun shines on the ripples of the water and, once again, Venice is *en fête.*

*Inside St Mark's Basilica right are the gleaming, massive piers and lofty cupolas which rise ninety-three feet above the level of the floor.*

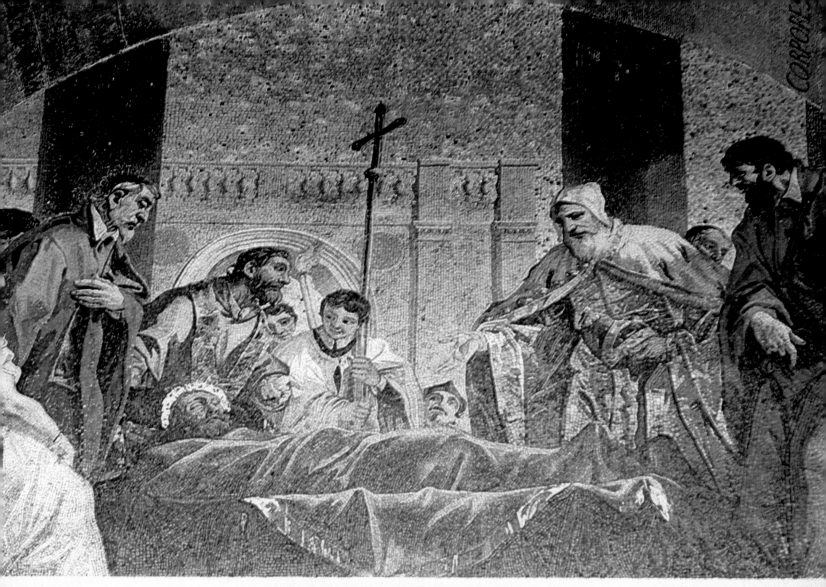

Within St Mark's Basilica, in the Dome of the Pentecost *left, the Divine Spirit descends upon the Apostles in the form of rivers of fire, while above* the mosaic in one of the lunettes *over the entrances to the Basilica reveals the Venetians paying homage to the body of St Mark; completed in 1728 by L. Ricci.*

*The solemn central doorway, with its rows of columns and antelamic carvings gracing the three great arches, is shown* right, *and below one of the mosaics of the spires which depicts 'The Resurrection of Christ', by Geatano, after drawings by Maffeo da Verona.*

*The moored gondolas overleaf stand sentinel in the misty morning air.*

Coducci's magnificent Clock Tower, dating from 1496/99, is sited in St Mark's Piazzetta and below is shown in detail the clockface with its astrological symbols.

The central arch of the Tower above marks the beginning of one of Venice's oldest streets, the Mercerie, which leads from St Mark's to the Rialto.

Dominating the foreground right is one of the four horses on the façade of St Mark's, plundered from Constantinople and placed here in the mid-fourteenth century.

Illustrated left are the winged lion, the emblem of Venice, and the Virgin and Child, gilded in copper, with 15th century designs in relief by the sculptor and goldsmith, Alessandro Leopardi. During the week of the Ascension the three Magi, preceded by an angel, emerge from one of the doors beside the Virgin, pass across the balcony and re-enter through the opposite door.

Superbly cast in bronze in 1497, by Ambrogio de la Anchora, is one of the two 'Moors' right, which have been striking the hours for more than four centuries.

# Streets Paved with Water

'VENICE is a wonderfully fine city,' the poet Shelley wrote home in 1818. 'It seems to have – and literally has – its foundations in the sea. The silent streets are paved with water, and you hear nothing but the dashing of the oars, and the occasional cries of the gondolieri.'

Until James Morris in *Venice* quoted Robert Benchley's cable home to America, on his first arrival in the city – 'Streets full of water. Please advise.' – Shelley's remark was probably more quoted than any other *bon mot* summing up Venice.

And it is the perfect summing up. Other cities – Amsterdam, Stockholm or Bangkok – may have streets and waterway intertwined, and Venice does have paved streets you can walk along, but the ones on which you must take a boat are essential to the city: it is the sea lapping round her ankles that makes Venice unique.

It is possible to take an unpoetical view of Venice's waterways. Long before twentieth-century tourists wrinkled their noses at the unexpected smell of a still backwater in the heat of summer, Lady Blessington, a less romantic visitor from England than Shelley, could write: 'The canal, too, over which our boat glided, bore evidence of the fallen state of the once proud Venice, for a green opaque slimy substance half-choaked its water, sending out a most unsavory smell, as the oars disturbed its unhealthy deposits.'

It is true that one may occasionally see a rat floating in a back canal, or a woman throwing a bag of household refuse into the canal beneath her window; but, on the whole, the smells are seldom encountered and the waterways of Venice are as clean and well-looked after as any elsewhere.

Having streets paved with water rather than asphalt or paving stones does give a city special problems, of course. In time of storm or heavy rain, the canals may rise over their banks and flood the ground floors, or cause the paving stones of St Mark's Square to disappear under inches, or even feet, of water. At such times, the Venetians wait for the waters to subside and then sweep out the remains fatalistically and with good humor: it is an accepted part of living in Venice.

To reach the foundations of a house to repair them, the canal outside the front door has to be drained. For the onlooker, the interesting thing about this is not what may be found on the bottom, but just how shallow the canals themselves generally are.

Most of the boats used on the canals are shallow-draught or, like the gondolas and rubbish and delivery barges, are flat-bottomed. When they need repairing, or when a Venetian gondolier or bargeman wants a new boat, they go to Venice's equivalent of any other city's garage workshop. Boat yards, or *squeri*, may be seen in various parts of Venice, the best-known of which is at San Trovaso, just off the Zattere. The San Trovaso yard is one of several still built of wood, as in generations past. They are busy places, piled with timber, tools, slipways and the hulls of unfinished or decayed boats.

At the height of her mercantile powers, Venice had such a traffic problem that strict rules had to be made governing where a boat might or might not be parked. There was a Magistrate of the Waters whose job it was to ensure that the traffic did not get snarled up, and that boats knew where they had to tie up to unload or take on cargo.

The Dalmations, or Slavs, were directed to tie up at the Riva, which eventually came to be called after them – the Riva degli Schiavoni; barges carrying sand or stone knew to make for the Incurabili; and timber ships from Cadore would unload at Misericordia or Barberia on the Fondamente Nuove.

In her heyday, Venice's greatest shipyard – and the greatest in the world – was the Arsenele. Boats are still built and repaired there, but the scale is nothing when compared with the sixteenth century, when it was probably the biggest workshop in the world.

It covered sixty acres to the east of St Mark's Square, and at any one time two thousand men would be working within the great walls, building and repairing more than a hundred galleys. They were using a conveyer belt system long before Henry Ford devised his assembly lines, and ships were all constructed to the same pattern so that ports as far apart as Southampton and Constantinople could hold spare parts to fit Venetian ships. A completed ship could be towed out of her dock, past store houses which would add their special equipment as she passed until, when she reached the Lagoon, she would be all ready to sail. Everyone in Venice connected with her navy or her merchant fleet knew exactly what they had to do when called out by the State.

Although the Arsenele is no longer of the vital importance to Venice it once was, Venice is still a major Mediterranean port. Look down any of the streets and canals that lead to the Giudecca Canal during the daytime, and the chances are that at the end of your vista will be a large ferry boat, merchant ship or naval vessel sailing past the Zattere on its way to the port of Venice.

Venice's main street is the Grand Canal, or Canalazza, as the Venetians call it. Despite its two and a half mile length, which cuts the city in half, it is crossed by only three bridges, the Accademia, the Rialto and the one by the railway station. Anyone wishing to cross the Grand Canal at any other point must call on one of the gondolas which will ferry passengers across for a small fee. Public transport along the Canal is by vaporetto, or water-bus, which can be boarded at several points on both sides of the Canal. The clatter of footsteps on the wooden landing stages of the water-bus remains for many one of the characteristic sound memories of Venice.

The smaller canals of the city are called *rio*, of which forty-five flow into the Grand Canal. Most of them are only about ten or fifteen feet wide, and cannot be negotiated by very large boats. Thus the water streets of Venice are alive with small gondolas, barges and brightly-painted boats; they are the taxis, delivery vans, refuse collectors and private cars of the modern city.

*The Rio dei Greci left, named after the Greek community which used to live here, has retained, since the time of the Renaissance, its Church of San Giorgio, with its slender, sloping bell-tower.*

*Equally beautiful by night or day – sun fills St Mark's Square* left, *while evening shadows lengthen under a midnight sky* these pages.

*One of the city's many regattas is shown* overleaf.

Standing on the right bank of the Grand Canal is Baldasarre Longhena's imposing Baroque masterpiece left, construction of which was started in 1630, following a decree by the senate to give thanks to the Virgin Mary at the end of the plague.

Throughout the city colorful awnings, flowers, statues and wrought iron-work transform even the most prosaic of buildings, adding luster to these charming Venetian scenes.

Venice contains over 400 bridges, some of which are illustrated on these pages, and possibly the most famous of all is the charming Baroque-inspired Bridge of Sighs above, designed by the architect Antonio Contino. It was across this bridge that prisoners would file, from their cells to the Palace of the Doge, to appear before the judges and, catching a glimpse of the lagoon probably 'sighed' for their lost freedom.

The white Palladian Church of San Giorgio and the antique Benedictine Convent shown overleaf, now belonging to the Cini Foundation, are sited on the island of San Giorgio Maggiore. Created by Andrea Palladio, the Church was constructed between 1565 and 1610, and the bell tower remodelled in 1791 by the Bolognese architect Benedetto Buratti, after the original tower had collapsed in 1773.

The distinctive Grand Canal, with its public transport water buses or 'vaporettos' right and lined with color-washed buildings is shown above and left, and below the picturesque fruit and vegetable market along the Ruga degli Orefici at the foot of the Rialto Bridge.

For centuries Venetians have built 'altana' at the top of their buildings where the washing may be hung to dry, or a small garden of pot plants created, and these can be seen amid the red tiled roof tops overleaf.

# Art in Venice

WALK round Venice today, and you feel that you are in the midst of the biggest art gallery in the world: houses, bridges, gondolas, even the very mooring poles in the canals, seem to have been designed as much for aesthetic pleasure as for practical use. It is partly a mirage, of course – the effect of sunlight reflected off water and on to walls, balconies and windows, softens, transforms and makes magical the most prosaic building.

Yet Venice does deserve her title of 'Jewel of the Adriatic', not just because of the effect the city as a whole has on most people – and there have been those who have been left completely cold by her opulence, thinking her vulgar and ostentatious – but because she really is one of the great monuments of European and world art, and because so many of her houses, palaces and squares contain works of art of great splendor and real genius.

Commentators are fond of saying that the Renaissance came late to Venice. Engrossed in their wars and mercantile expansion, Venice's merchants and statesmen had no time for the artistic revolution that was transforming Siena, Florence, Padua and other Italian cities. They were content that Venice's greatest artistic successes should be in the use she made of mosaics in churches and palaces. The work of masters from Ravenna and Byzantium had ensured that the Cathedral of Torcello and St Mark's Basilica were both alive with the gleam of gold and the rich imagery of the mosiac-covered walls.

It is true that when the Renaissance flowered in Venice it took a form different from that in other Italian states. The great painters – the Bellinis, Giorgione, Titian, Carpaccio – seemed concerned less with portraying the glories of individuals, whether God, saints or man, than with recording details of a domestic nature, or urging the beauties and strength of nature. Carpaccio's vast series of paintings of the Life of St Ursula, in the Accademia, is full of domestic detail which makes it of as much interest to the social historian as to the art lover; Giovanni Bellini's superb portrait of the Doge Leonardo Loredan, now in London's National Gallery, depicts the nature of the man himself rather than the glory of the super-human ruler of Venice; Giorgione's *The Tempest* has nature as the subject of the painting, not just as a decorative background.

Another major difference between the Venetian and other schools of Italian painting lies in the Venetians' use of color. Perhaps it was the influence of the mosaics of earlier centuries and the special Venetian inter-play of light and water, but the paintings of the Venetian artists were notable for the brilliance and luminosity of their color. The great art historian, Bernard Berenson, said that the Venetians used color with 'exquisite tact… Seldom cold and rarely too warm, their coloring…acts like music upon the moods'.

Today, the work of the painters of the Venetian Renaissance can be seen splendidly displayed in great palaces or hidden away in dark corners of apparently insignificant churches. Tintoretto, especially, has left examples of his work all over Venice, dotted about in churches in all parts of the city, hung in glory in the Doge's Palace, and assembled in over-whelming array in the Scuola di San Rocco. The Scuola, one of five charitable schools in Venice, gave Tintoretto an annual pension in exchange for three paintings a year. His vast *Crucifixion* stretches forty feet across one wall of an assembly room in the Scuola.

The doges were great patrons of artists, commissioning acres of paintings to cover the walls of the Doge's Palace with pictorial records of Venetian triumphs. Giovanni Bellini and Carpaccio were ordered by the Senate to work 'continuously and every day' on their work in the Palace. Painters, architects, sculptors, engravers and decorators all contributed to the creation of one of the most richly decorated palaces in the world.

The greatest treasure store of painting in Venice is the Accademia Gallery. 'Allow at least two hours for the Gallery: even the selection given below runs to 93 pictures,' says a recent guide to Venice, advising its readers to have a cup of coffee first. Well, two hours would give the casual visitor a quick run through, but a life-time would hardly suffice for anyone seriously interested in discovering the glories of the Accademia.

On its walls are some of the finest examples of the art of the Venetian painters of the Renaissance and of Venetian art's second flowering in the eighteenth century. It is a splendidly-planned gallery, well lit and airy, and worth several visits.

One vaporetto stop up the Grand Canal from the Accademia is the Palazzo Rezzonico, once owned by Robert Browning's son, Pen, and scene of the poet's death in 1889. The palace now houses a museum of eighteenth century furniture and paintings.

Started at the beginning of the seventeenth century and finished in the middle of the eighteenth, this palace, like so many others along the Grand Canal, is a splendid example of how in Venetian architecture, as in Venetian painting, the basic form is one of pure and simple lines. The same observation applies to the fifteenth-century Ca' d'Oro, another Grand Canal palace which houses an art gallery. The Ca' d'Oro has a facade completely covered with polychrome marble, a columned portico, loggias and interwoven arches – a typical example of the elaborate Venetian Gothic style of its period. Yet, beneath the ornamentation, the basic form is simple and straightforward.

If art in Venice has pleased the eye for centuries, it has also pleased the ear. A recent revival of interest in the music of the baroque period has drawn attention to Venice's place in the musical life of the Renaissance and post-Renaissance period.

Monteverdi was thirty years in charge of music at St Mark's and held the title of Master of the Music of the Republic; Vivaldi spent most of his adult life at the Conservatorio of the Pietà, one of four charitable schools in Venice where orphans were trained for careers in music. The first public opera house, as distinct from private houses paid for by noble patrons of music, was opened in Venice early in the seventeenth century. The famous Fenice Theater, built in the 1790s and possessing one of the loveliest interiors of any theater in the world, has seen the premieres of many operas.

Monteverdi and Vivaldi can frequently be heard in Venice today, as concerts of their music are given regularly in the courtyard of the Doge's Palace in the summer.

*Dating from the 8th century, the Church of San Moisé left was originally built to honor San Vittore, but was reconstructed in the 10th century by Moisé Venier.*

*The Cavalli Franchetti Palace overleaf is considered to be one of the most beautiful examples of 15th century Gothic architecture.*

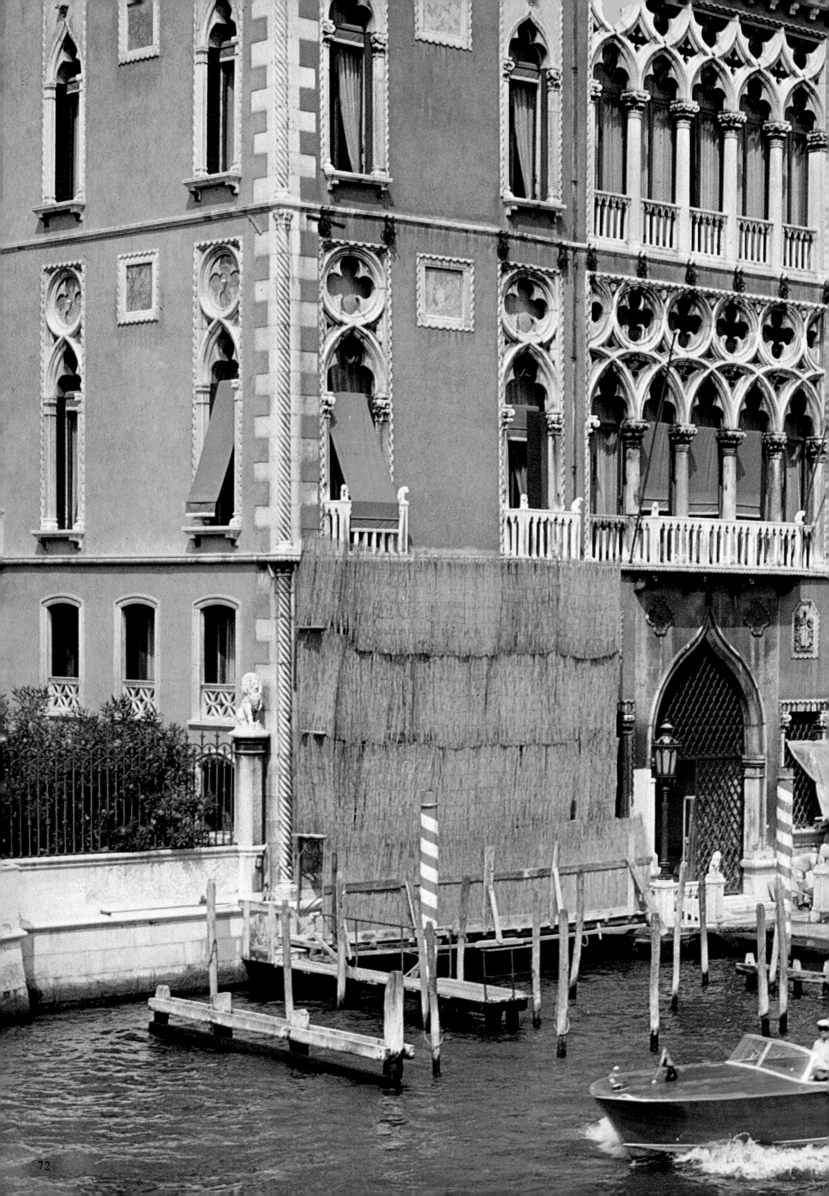

From the basin of San Marco can be seen the political, civil and religious heart of Venice above and far left, *and* right, *shrouded in mist, the Church of San Giorgio Maggiore.*

*The white cupola of the Church of Santa Maria della Salute rises over the graceful houses* above right, *with, at the very mouth of the Grand Canal the Dogana da Mar (Customs House), its shimmering, gilded sphere, symbolizing fortune shown in detail* left. *Built by Giovanni Benoni, in 1677, it was here that at one time goods were unloaded and tolls paid.*

*Overlooking the wharf is the splendid façade of the Doge's Palace* overleaf, *the flight of steps in the foreground leading to the Ponte della Paglia (Bridge of Straw) across the Rio di Palazzo.*

# Islands of the Lagoon

VENICE sits almost in the center of a lagoon thirty-five miles long and seven miles wide at its widest point. Around its shores are villages and towns and dotted about its waters are islands which have been part of the history of Venice itself. The group of islands – Rivo Alto, or Rialto – which make up present-day Venice were not the early settlers' first choice of refuge when they fled to the Lagoon from the mainland. Legend has it that the Bishop of Altinum was told by God Himself to move his See to the Lagoon, and that God indicated the island of Torcello as the right spot.

Torcello is one of the northern-most islands in the Lagoon, a few minutes away by boat from the delightful island of Burano. Even the least-imaginative visitor to Torcello feels there an atmosphere quite different from the liveliness and color of Venice. It is an atmosphere compounded of a lingering memory of things past, of days of bustle and power long since disappeared and of marshes and swamps once filled with the dreaded scourge of malaria – an atmosphere which even the hottest sunshine of the brightest summer day cannot quite dispel.

Once Torcello was covered with a network of streets and canals, its houses were home to a population of something like 20,000 people, and its churches were filled with worshippers. It gradually fell into a state of neglect when the government of Venice was moved to the Rialto, and the process was accelerated in the eighteenth century because of its reputation for being malarial. People came from the main town to search among its ruins for building materials and stones for the new city, and the old Torcello disappeared into memory, leaving its traces in paintings of old Venice which show it dominating the skyline.

Today, Torcello is a tourist attraction, but it has dignity in its solitude which makes it more memorable than many another 'attraction'. Sitting in a group amongst green fields and gardens are the superb Cathedral of Santa Maria Assunta, its square brick campanile, the Church of Santa Fosca, a strange stone throne, and two small palaces. Standing slightly aside from this group is the well-known Locanda Cipriani, an off-shoot of Harry's Bar in Venice, which offers a restaurant good enough to have attracted such famous people to its tables as Ernest Hemingway, Pablo Picasso and Winston Churchill.

Torcello's Cathedral is older than St Mark's in Venice. Although it has been restored and altered at various times, it has kept much of the form it had when it was built in 639 in the style of Ravenna and Byzantium. Outside, it is built simply of brick with roofs of curved tiles. Inside, it has an impressive array of mosaics, some of which date back to the eighth-century masters of Ravenna, and some of which were completed in the fourteenth century.

The 'Universal Judgement' mosaic inside the Cathedral is stupendous both in size and execution, but even more memorable is the mosaic figure, high in the apse, of the Virgin and Child; standing alone against a gold background, spare, tall and immensely sad, the Virgin with her tear-stained face has rightly been called one of the most vivid and spontaneous works of art in Venice.

Burano is so different from Torcello that it is hard to remember that only five minutes by boat separates one from the other. Venice's center for the delicate and intricate business of lace-making, Burano is also a down-to-earth and immensely colorful fishing community. The walks beside her canals may be piled with fishing nets and cork floats, the canals themselves alive with fishing boats and fishermen. In front of many houses, groups of women sit and make lace. The houses themselves – simple, flat-fronted and unadorned – have been painted in vivid colors, so that squares of pink, red, ocher, blue, yellow and rich chestnut line the canals and squares in a warm and welcoming panorama.

Girls are taught the business of lace-making at the Scuola dei Merletti, which welcomes visitors. Lace can be bought there, and it is expensive, of course; a fact which has bothered many commentators on the Venetian scene. The girls who make the lace are learners and paid very little. They may be ruining their eyesight so that others can be odorned in the exquisitely delicate results of their labors.

At least the product of the work is beautiful. The same cannot always be said of the products of the island of Murano. Glass has been the business of Murano since the thirteenth century when all the businesses of the glass-makers were moved away from the center of Venice because their furnaces had caused too many fires in the city. A visit to a glass factory is a high spot on many tourist itineraries. The actual making of the glass items is a process well worth watching, but the final products set out in the factory showrooms are generally garish, over-adorned and frankly vulgar. There is a glass museum to be visited, and one lovely church, that of St Donato, which is almost as old as St Mark's and has a curiously undulating floor, caused by subsidence over the centuries.

These islands lie to the north of Venice. At the southernmost end of the lagoon lies Chioggia. To get there by boat from Venice one must pass several other islands used to accommodate the less happy aspects of modern life: an island for the tuberculosis hospital, one for contagious diseases, and one each for the insane of each sex. (Venice's cemetery is also an island – St Michele to the north of the city.)

Chioggia, like Burano, is a fishing center but the town is less attractive than the island and has a neglected air, though connoisseurs of fish say that some of the sea food restaurants are excellent. Chioggia has played its part in the history of Venice, for it was here in 1380 that the Genoese surrendered to the Venetian fleet, leaving to Venice the mastery of the Adriatic.

*Erected on the site of the original Bell Tower which collapsed in 1902, the present structure right was inaugurated in 1912, on St Mark's Day and is known to the Venetians as the 'paron de casa' (master of the house). Surmounting the tower is a gilded angel which moves to indicate the wind's direction.*

*Deserted except for pigeons and a solitary street cleaner is the normally bustling St Mark's Square overleaf.*

The superb Doge's Palace, with its four-lobed traceries of the Foscari Loggia left, contains within its courtyard illustrated right and bottom center, two bronze well-curbs sculpted by Niccolò dei Conti and Alfonso Alberghetti.

On a corner overlooking the Rio di Palazzo is the sculpture depicting 'The Drunkenness of Noah' below and beyond it can be seen the Bridge of Sighs.

The magnificent Staircase of the Giants right, designed by Antonio Rizzo, was so named because of the enormous statues of Mars and Neptune which stand on either side of the stairway crest. The Doge, on election, was traditionally crowned at the head of the stairs in the presence of the people and dignitaries of the Republic.

The traditional gondola overleaf embarks on a tour of the city and her islands, while on page 86 can be seen the congested waterway, massed with boats.

# Daily Life in Venice

'THE fairest place of all the citie,' wrote Thomas Coryat in 1611, 'is the Piazza...Here you may both see all manner of fashions of attire, and heare all the languages of Christendome, besides those that are spoken by the barbarous Ethnickes; the frequencies of people being so great twise a day... a man may vary properly call it rather Orbis then Urbis forum...'

Three and a half centuries later, the Piazza of St Mark on a summer's day contains just such a scene as Coryat described. It may well be filled with people of all races, colors and creeds, just as impressed by the admirable and incomparable beauty of the architecture as was Coryat. It is likely to be well attended by Venetians, too, for St Mark's is the main meeting place of their city, not just a tourist attraction.

In the summer Venetians spend much of their time out of doors. Their houses, which may face narrow back streets and canals from which the sun is excluded for much of the day, are inclined to be dark inside and, anyway, where better to be than outdoors on a warm summer's day?

Outdoors may mean just a chair or two brought out into the sunshine from the house, or it may mean sitting on one's own roof. For centuries, Venetian houses have had *altana* built on their roofs. The washing may be hung up to dry there, or a small garden of geraniums and other pot plants created in its shelter. It is also a fine private place to sunbathe or dry one's hair. In Renaissance days, the women of Venice would induce their hair to turn that glorious copper color to be seen in the paintings of Titian by sitting in the sun with their hair pulled through a large brim with no crown. One of the most famous of Carpaccio's paintings shows two women sitting, splendidly dressed and playing with their pet dogs, on the altana of their house.

Outdoors in Venice can also mean a meeting of friends and family in a restaurant or café in one of the city's many small squares. The evening aperitif is an important ritual for many, and the children may come too, to play in the square and among the café tables while the adults talk and pass the time of day. Most cafés and restaurants bring tables out into the street or square in the summer. Sometimes, the street is so narrow that passers-by must walk among the diners to get to their destination.

Above the heads of diners and passers-by, the buildings may jut out, making the streets even narrower. This kind of building projection is called a *barbacano* and, far from being a haphazard answer to lack of space, has been a strictly-controlled method of giving Venetians more living room. In the days of the magistrates, there was one magistrate whose job was to plan and regulate the building of barbacani.

Many commentators have been surprised by the number of Venetians who confess to seldom, if ever, leaving the part of the city in which they live. They see no reason to go to the other side of the city, when their own area has everything they need and, anyway, is far the best part of Venice to be in. Thus, the pace of life of the average Venetian is that of the village, rather than the bustling city.

The city has been divided for centuries into six *sestieri*, called San Marco, Castello, Cannaregio, Santa Croce, San Polo and Dorsoduro. Buildings are numbered after a system, incomprehensible to the outsider, according to sestieri, not street. Thus, one's house will not be numbered 17 Calle del Pistor, but Dorsoduro 5745 – and a stranger looking for it could walk up and down streets and alleys for a long time before finding it.

Local shops are run by people the Venetians know, and with whom they can have long discussions over the quality of the goods on sale; their fruit and vegetables may be handed to them in cornets of brown paper made up on the spot by the shop-keeper, rather than in more sophisticated plastic bags; their bread may be delivered by a boy who walks the streets with it in a long basket pannier slung over his shoulders. The death of a relative will be announced on a black-edged card placed in a local shop window, rather than simply in the impersonal columns of a newspaper. The death may even be announced on posters stuck to walls.

The custom of the black-edged card is common in Italy, but unique to Venice is the way of conducting a funeral there. The Venetian hearse is a boat, available in a variety of styles depending on how much the relatives of the deceased feel able to pay. A funeral becomes another Venetian pageant, somber with plumes, brass fittings and flowers. And all funerals end up at the cemetery on the island of San Michele – peaceful, calm and lined with cypress trees.

For the visitor to Venice, one of the best ways of seeing the daily life of the city at work is to visit the great market which lies near the Rialto Bridge. It is actually several markets; to one is brought at dawn the results of the night's fishing on the Lagoon and out in the Adriatic. Fish and shell fish in great variety and color are laid out for buyers to look at, prod and discuss at length before purchasing. In the fruit and vegetable markets is sold an enormous variety of goods which come to Venice from the surrounding mainland. Among the buyers will be old ladies in the traditional black clothing, careful housewives feeling each apple before putting it in a bag, nuns with graceful headdresses, tourists in straw gondoliers' boaters – all jostling together under the arcades and the canvas awnings of the dozens of stalls. It is a rich and colorful scene, full of sights and scents to please all the senses.

*A 14th century palace, at one time the private residence of Doge Dandolo, the Hotel Danieli (CIGA Hotels) left now provides luxurious accomodation for the visitor to Venice.*

Tourists throng St Mark's Square above and left, while below can be seen one of many photographers ever anxious to capture the glittering beauty of the Basilica's façade below left, its domes and minarets soaring upwards into an azure sky.

As dusk falls over the Palace of the Doge overlooking the Riva degli Schiavoni right, lamps shine in the misty evening air, where lovers stroll hand in hand and look out towards the basin of San Marco, in this city made for romance.

The bright lights of the restaurants and bars, the convivial atmosphere of the cafés, and the artists who can still be seen at work throughout the city, act as a reminder that Venice is not purely a museum city of ancient buildings and silent gondolas.

To the north of Venice lies the island of Burano *overleaf, characterized by low, modest houses with vividly colored façades and canals alive with flat bottomed fishing boats.*

First published in Great Britain 1979 by Colour Library International Ltd.
© Illustrations: Colour Library International Ltd.
Colour separations by La Cromolito, Milan, Italy.
Display and text filmsetting by Focus Photoset, London, England.
Printed and bound by Rieusset, Barcelona, Spain.
I.S.B.N. 0-8317-9125-X Library of Congress Catalogue Card N.º 79-2060
Published in the United States of America by Mayflower Books, Inc., New York City
Published in Canada by Wm. Collins and Sons, Toronto